MW00809935

Christian Archy

David Alan Black

Energion Publications

P. O. Box 841
Gonzalez, FL 32560

http://energionpubs.com
pubs@energion.com

Cover Design: Jason Neufeld, jasonneufelddesign.com

ISBN-10: 1-893729-77-X
ISBN-13: 978-1-893729-77-3

Library of Congress Control Number: 2009939435

Dedication

To the memory of Jacques Ellul

CONTENTS

From the Editors vii

Preface ix

Acknowledgments xii

Chapter 1: Introduction 1

Chapter 2: The Major Tenets of Christian Archy 5

Chapter 3: Some Implications of Christian Archy 11

Chapter 4: Church and Kingdom 17

Chapter 5: The Power of the Powerless 27

Chapter 6: Conclusion 33

For Further Reading 37

Topics and Persons Index 41

Scripture Index 43

From the Editors

The Areopagus is a hill in Athens that was once the meeting place of a Greek council. Paul preached on that hill while visiting Athens, presenting the Gospel to the Athenian council and converting one of them (Acts 17). It thus provides an excellent name for this series of booklets that examines important issues in understanding Christian beliefs and developing sound Christian practice. Each booklet is intentionally short – less than 80 pages in length – and provides an academically sound and biblically rooted examination of a particular question about doctrine or practice or an area of basic Christian belief.

The Areopagus series is orthodox in doctrine but not bound to the doctrinal statements of any denomination. It is both firm in conviction and irenic in tone. Authors have been chosen for their ability to understand a topic in depth and present it clearly.

Each book is rigorous in scholarship because we believe the church deserves no less. Yet the volumes are accessible in style as we also believe that there are many pastors and laypersons in the church who desire to think deeply and critically about the issues that confront the church today in its life and mission in the world.

In keeping with these convictions, the authors in this series are either professors who are also actively involved in ministry, pastors who have not only thought through the issues but whose ministry has been guided by their convictions, or laypersons whose faith and commitment to the lordship of Jesus Christ and his church have contributed to the Great Commission Jesus gave to all of his followers (Matt. 28:18-20).

The *Areopagus Critical Christian Issues* series is not only meant to help the church think differently. We hope that those who read its volumes will be different, for the Gospel is about the transformation of the whole person – mind, heart, and soul.

We take the words of the apostle Paul seriously when he says to the Athenians that God "has fixed a day on which he will have the world judged in righteousness by a man whom he has appointed; and of this he has given assurance to all by raising him from the dead" (Acts 17:31).

Allan R. Bevere

David Alan Black

Preface

The older I get, the more I realize what I don't know. This is a liberating insight. Authors never reach an end to conversations and debates, nor should they.

In the following pages I attempt to reopen an old debate. Neither a professor of philosophy, nor of theology, I attempt little more than brushing lightly those areas normally reserved for specialists. My thesis is simple: I argue that the economic and political necessities of our time are best served when God's kingdom comes first. The doctrine of Christ crucified for us puts an end to religion as power. The last word in human affairs is represented by a man hanging on a cross (1 Cor. 2:2).

In this book I have attempted to listen attentively to the New Testament, even to what at first blush does not suit me. I have sought to expound the distinctive contribution of the New Testament to the theme of the kingdom of God – what it is, how to enter it, and how to walk worthily of it as its citizens. The character of this kingdom is widely different from what is commonly envisaged today. Its glory is revealed only through suffering – a point that Jesus' disciples, then and now, have been slow to understand. This truth has tremendous implications for church life. The kingdom of God is in no way imperialistic. It has no political ambitions. It conquers not by force but by love. It is this humble characteristic of the kingdom that is a stumbling block to so many today. Christ's claim to our total allegiance is one we seek to avoid at all costs. But there is only one way to victory and peace, and that is the way of the Lamb:

> They follow the Lamb wherever he goes. They were bought from among humanity, the firstfruits to God and to the Lamb. And in their mouths was found no lie (Rev. 14:4-5; all translations in this book are my own).

This understanding of the kingdom is good news for everyone. The rule of God has been inaugurated. The time has been fulfilled. And the work is all God's.

I hope that this book will be the first in a series of short studies that encourage fresh discovery of and lively debate with important critical issues in the church. The aim is not to produce monographs in the technical sense but a useable series of pamphlets with guidance at essential points. This explains the brevity of the present work. As this book goes to press it is my fervent prayer that it will awaken new interest in the subject of the kingdom of God and stimulate believers of all denominations to reflect more deeply on the purpose for which the church exists.

Acknowledgments

In everything I write I discover how much I owe to my teachers. I must single out here the lecturers at Basel under whom I had the privilege of sitting: Bo Reicke, Markus Barth, Jan Milic Lockman, Martin Anton Schmidt, and Bernhard Wyss. Most important of all I should mention a mentor who, via his publications, has been my discussion partner for several months now. No one has caused me greater joy in my studies of the New Testament than Jacques Ellul, and it is to his memory that this book is dedicated.

This volume is a natural outgrowth of its predecessor, *The Jesus Paradigm*, also published by Energion Publications. I want to say thank you to its owner, Henry Neufeld, who has worked closely with me on formatting and design to produce books that are not only visually pleasant but that deal with issues that confront today's increasingly complex and broken world.

Finally, I want to thank my fellow pilgrims all over the world – from Bucharest to Beijing – who have been an anvil on which I have forged my ideas. The kingdom is truly universal in scope, and I am grateful to have witnessed its expressions among many different nations of the world.

Chapter 1:

Introduction

There is perhaps no clearer example of the church's misguided appropriation of the world than the god of nationalism. Instead of simply following Jesus, whose kingdom is marked by powerless love, we have attempted to use Christianity to support worldly power. And this means that the church has lost its way – a transgression that carries with it an obligation on the part of every Christian to find his or her way back to the correct path. Experience has shown that once the church has become just another worldly "archy" (power), once it has allowed itself to be subverted by politics, it has achieved a "victory" at the expense of the Gospel.

This is the message of two profound Christian thinkers whose writings impacted a previous generation of Jesus followers. It has only been recently that I added the works of Jacques Ellul and Vernard Eller to my library shelves, and their contribution to what they call "Christian Anarchy" has played no little role in the writing of my latest book, *The Jesus Paradigm*. Picking up on something Kierkegaard once said, these philosopher-theologians remind us that the Gospel is something intolerable, for it requires us to renounce the illusions, the misplaced hopes, and the blind cul-de-sacs of religious archys. "Christendom," wrote Kierkegaard, "is an effort of the human race to go back to walking on all fours, to get rid of Christianity, to do it knavishly under the pretext that this is Christianity, claiming that it is Christianity perfected" (cited in Ellul, *The Subversion of Christianity*, p. 1). This is not all. "The Christianity of Christendom," continues Kierkegaard, "transforms Christianity into something entirely different from what it is in the New Testament, yea, into exactly the opposite; and this is the Christianity of Christendom, of us men."

The tragedy is that Christians have freely chosen this course of action. They have voluntarily opted for Christendom over Christianity. They have willingly forsaken the Holy Spirit for holy orders, the Body of Christ for a body of worldly ideals, the kingdom of heaven for the kingdoms of this world. As I argue in my new book, I am convinced that this "subversion of Christianity" (the title of one of Ellul's books), this matter of putting our petty gods above Christ, has caused the church to *totally* miss its way. It is only when we exalt *Christus Victor*, when we believe in Christ crucified and risen again, when we acknowledge that whatever substitutions for Christianity we have allowed are nothing but false Christianities, that we can make any headway.

The description of our problem – and its distinctly biblical solution as set forth by Ellul and Eller – though obvious to anyone who has read their works, is unfortunately not well known today or, if it is, is rejected partly because it is known as "Christian *Anarchy*," a term that to many has an exceedingly negative connotation. It is here, of course, that Christian theologians have a major role to play in fleshing out these works, but many have not understood that role because (in my estimation) they do not get beyond the nomenclature to the substance of Christian Anarchy. Some have even lent their support to the foolish and utopian ideas of Christendom, seeking the goodness of the Lord in the "wonder-working power" of the American people, to paraphrase a recent U.S. president. Such pom-pom waving allegiance to the American flag and U.S.-style democracy is no more than one of the ways in which Christendom seeks to "transform Christianity into something entirely different from what it is in the New Testament" (as Kierkegaard said). When the Christian church behaves like this, and when its theologians go along with it, it utterly fails to be the light of the world and the salt of the earth, overcoming evil with good.

There is, therefore, a need for the church to rediscover its failure to plant the cross at the heart of its identity as church, and thus for the church to be reborn through the seed of evangelical truth. By way of impudent generalization, I will attempt in this book to describe the way forward. It seems to me, from my reading of Ellul and especially Eller, that we can discern three processes, three movements in this symphony of truth that I will now call "Christian *Archy.*" I think that we have in this symphony an explanation of the astonishing change that brought Christendom into existence out of Christianity, even though the biblical revelation lends the exchange absolutely no support. From this point on, then, let us briefly examine Christian Archy and see whether it can help us to better understand how the church has been subverted and how it might be reconstituted along biblical lines. It is absurd to think that my synopsis is either sufficient or efficient for this to occur. At the very least, my hope is that my audience will feel compelled to "take up and read" for themselves the provocative works I am merely trying to summarize here (see *For Further Reading*).

Chapter 2:

The Major Tenets of Christian Archy

As I see it, there are three.

1. In the first place, the Gospel is concerned with the kingdom of God and only with the kingdom of God. This kingdom cannot, therefore, be equated with any human archy, be that archy left wing or right wing, liberal or conservative, revolutionary or anti-revolutionary, Roman Catholic, Orthodox, or Protestant. The Archy of God is intent on reconciling adversaries instead of creating them. Politically, Christian Archy rejects the partisan power contest. At its heart lies the cross and the self-givingness of love. All worldly archys are therefore antithetical to the Archy of God, including "good" archys that rely upon an unfounded confidence in the moral competency of humans and that seek to impose their "right" upon people they believe to be "wrong." Again, I know I am oversimplifying, but these characteristics are precisely found, for example, in the first chapter of Eller's *Christian Anarchy*

2. The second and no less astonishing feature of Christian Archy is the contention that the ultimate

victory of God's Archy will take place without any assistance or support from the efforts of human archys of any kind, including those of Christendom, whether of the Christian Right or the Christian Left (see Eller, *Christian Anarchy*, chapter 2). Eller maintains that human efforts to establish the kingdom of God have absolutely no biblical or theological foundations. Christ's Archy has *nothing whatsoever* to do with "holy causes, programs, and ideologies that will effect the social reformation of society" (*Christian Anarchy*, p. 25). Absolutely nothing! Politics, argues Eller, is one such false messiah, though any movement or ideology that takes the place of the cross belongs under the same rubric and merits the same appraisal. This tendency to supplant the cross of Christ with human solutions (including "holy" ones) and to anoint them with near-divine status is called "arky faith" by Eller. ("Arky" is Eller's preferred spelling of "archy.") Arky faith is present whenever one attempts to use piety to force its version of "justice" into place as *the* solution to "injustice." Writes Eller (*Christian Anarchy*, p. 27):

> I am convinced that there are many Christians (of both the left and right) who, as individuals, are quite modest, humble, and of realistic self-image – but who, then, proceed to satisfy their lust for power, their delusions of grandeur, and their sense of self-righteousness through the holy arkys

with which they identify. Asserting their "just cause" becomes a psychological disguise for asserting themselves; thus they find Christian justification for the sense of power to which all of us are tempted.

This does not mean, continues Eller, that human archys do not exist or are irrelevant. It is simply to insist that God's Archy is not of this world – which means that, as Christians, it is unnecessary to fight the archys, compete with them, or recognize any merit on their part. In fact, Christian Archy is completely indifferent to human archys, whether they be communist, pacifist, liberal, democratic, libertarian, revolutionary, etc. What matters is that the church be the church, refusing to sacralized earthly archys and even itself. God does not need our worldly systems (dogmatics, philosophy, science, politics) or even our "centers for cultural transformation" to bring about societal reformation. Jesus alone suffices.

3. Precisely because the church has abandoned its apolitical message, a third and final dimension to Christian Archy must be mentioned, namely that no worldly archy has any actual power or ultimate significance (see Eller, *Christian Anarchy*, chapter 3). "Christianity started out as a completely anarchic ekklesia and then drifted into churchly arkydom," writes Eller (p. 52). By "churchly arkydom" he means any worldly archy that replaces Christian Archy or that

vies for our attention, examples being Christian feminism, liberation theology, and social revolution. In Christ's kingdom, archys based on gender, class, and social standing are completely irrelevant. Christians are called upon to rely exclusively on the Holy Spirit, who "gives hope where all is despair, the strength to endure in the midst of disaster, perspicacity not to fall victim to seduction, the ability to subvert in turn all the powers that are involved" (Ellul, *The Subversion of Christianity*, p. 190). With reference specifically to churchly archys, Eller notes that an ekklesia "is still a totally anarchic concept; no hint of arkydom is involved" (*Christian Anarchy*, p. 50). In the church, therefore, there are no human actors who function as special, anointed agents capable either of representing God to men or representing men to God, nor can any single individual speak entirely for God as *pater familias* (pope, patriarch, priest, bishop, pastor, etc.). Is this perspective anticlerical? Decidedly so, if by this is meant that ecclesiastical leaders should think of themselves self-sufficient and able to disregard their fellow Christians. Decidedly not, if by this is meant the conviction that all the brothers and sisters are able to admonish and teach one another in the Lord, being one Body and one Bread and of one mind.

And so, in Christ, the archys of the world are definitively desacralized, eliminated, and vanquished. This is the essential upshot (as I see it) of Christian

The Major Tenets of Christian Archy

Archy, which implies a radical reconstitution of what is truly sacral in God's eyes.

Chapter 3:

Some Implications of Christian Archy

It is evident that each of the three movements we have discussed, and the symphony of truth they form, entail a constant struggle between the church's desire to desacralize itself and its desire to engage in practices that are totally incompatible with the Archy of Christ. We may recall the tendencies of the Magisterial Reformers to legitimize the power of the establishment archys and even to use the magistrate's "sword" to gain for them legal standing. Eller tackles this aspect of the problem by mentioning explicitly the sixteenth-century Anabaptists, who resisted "impositional pressure" (*Christian Anarchy*, p. 32) to advance the Gospel and who placed no faith whatsoever in human archys to establish the kingdom. (In my new book I devote an entire chapter to these Anabaptists.) In these movements the Free Church element was very strong. The idea that God's revolution could *by force* be manipulated to a desired end was rejected by the Anabaptists except for a revolutionary faction that unfortunately held to an "arky faith" (*Christian Anarchy*, p. 33).

It is a platitude to say that archy faith predominates in Christian circles today, mixing the profane with the sacred, and confusing the end and the means. As long as the church looks for an objective outside itself, which it tries to obtain by very great human effort, it forsakes its calling to be the instrument of God. One such "churchly archy," in my opinion, is the homeschool movement in Christian circles, which tends to greatly oversimplify moral decision making: homeschooling is good, government education is evil. Once again, Christianity has been subverted, and a process of earthly archy has developed. This is the well-known mechanism whereby one avoids a troublesome dilemma by projecting an ideal. The result is a tragic substitution of reason for revelation.

Now, I do not deny that there are very valid and persuasive reasons to homeschool one's children (my wife and I homeschooled through high school). I am simply saying that this is a makeshift that can easily substitute morality for the Gospel and exalt law over faith, hope, and love. This is why I do not agree with the Christian homeschool *agenda* (please note the italicized word) when it argues that the New Testament requires parents to educate their children at home and when it advocates sociopolitical reasons and explanations. For the life of me, I can't find anything in the Gospels or Epistles of the white-hatted homeschooler pitted against the black-hatted public schooler. No, the Gospel has in fact said nothing about what external form the education of our children should take, except that Christian parents are accountable for raising their children "in the nurture and admonition of the Lord."

There is here a kind of fundamentalism at work that attempts to achieve uniformity at all costs. Differences in the interpretation of Eph. 6:1-4 now become inadmissible, and annual denominational conventions even attempt to pass resolutions condemning all government-sponsored education. As I see it (and this is merely my opinion), the crux is that the Christian homeschool movement tends to promise what it cannot deliver: children who grow up to become mature Christians. My guess is that anyone who has raised children that have turned out to be sincere, obedient Jesus followers will say that it depended completely upon God's grace rather than upon any formal *method* of education. Had Eller himself written about this topic (which, as far as I know, he never did), I imagine he might have said something like this: "We dare not declare, *in principle*, homeschooling to be preferable to government schooling in all cases. Each family, and each case, is *relative* to its own merits. Christian Archy not only allows us to give God alone absolute loyalty but frees us to treat relative choices as the human relatives they are." Now, if we extend this same principle to questions of curriculum (Bob Jones versus Rod and Staff?) and methodology (classical versus modern foreign languages?), I think we will arrive at the heart of Christian Archy.

Certainly, what has been said about the Christian homeschool movement (again, I am sympathetic to homeschooling as such) can also be said about any other Christian "reformist" movement (patriarchy, agrarianism, age-integration, etc.). The trouble is that such moralizing can be done sheerly in the flesh. We can get so caught up in the idea of raising modern knights or returning to the land or asserting male headship when oftentimes all that is actually happening is that our little archy is becoming more and more impressed by its own importance as a revolutionary cause. I am not enumerating here an abstract or theoretical view of things. The dangers lurking in our false panaceas have been fully proven in our day. A similar situation arises whenever one equates the Gospel with right-wing politics – or, for that matter, left-wing politics. "It is the same mistake either way," observes Eller. "The only question is whether there ever has been any human arky – church, state, cause, group, or whatever – that has merited recognition as God's chosen instrument of human salvation" (*Christian Anarchy*, p. 31).

This fact is not always sufficiently realized. Ellul has a very strong statement in this regard: "All this is a tragic result of the substitution of morality for revelation that for two thousand years has been one of the aspects of the perversion of the will of God" (*The Subversion of Christianity*, p. 94). If Christian Archy means anything, it means that all the "answers" proposed by humanity to achieve the ends proposed by God are useless and inadequate. Every earthly archy is illusory, and keeps us tied to an outlook we should be abandoning. This simply means that one cannot seek first the kingdom of God and at the same time seek "all these things" *in addition to the kingdom.*

The Enemy of the church always seeks to turn it aside from the cross in order to make it follow its own way. At various times in its turbulent history, the church has been socialist or communist, liberal or fundamentalist, political or anti-political. It has espoused the social gospel, revolution (of both the violent and non-violent types), egalitarianism, complementarianism, classlessness, class distinction, colonization, and communism. In each case the church has tended to become part of the problem rather than part of the solution. Writes Ellul, "[The church] is no more than one of the forms in which the will of the world is expressed, and actually it is helping the world to realize its own ends. It no longer represents the power of the action of God in the world" (*The Presence of the Kingdom*, p. 125). While earthly archys might have a certain value from a purely human perspective, they are inevitably compromised and, says Ellul, "these 'compromises' have turned out badly for the church" (p. 126).

Christian Archy

It seems that our steel is fatally flawed after all. It is only in Jesus Christ, the Originator and Finalizer of faith, that we have any possibility of salvation. In reality, *the Gospel is the only source of personal, familial, and societal renewal.* What matters, then, is not that we lose ourselves in futile political or social agitation. What matters is that we recognize in the incarnation of Christ, and in his death and resurrection, that God was intervening in the course of human history to give us not only eternal life but an abundant life every day. There is now only one response we can give – calling all men and women into a relationship with God through this same Jesus.

Chapter 4:

Church and Kingdom

It is clear now that the goal of Christianity is to advance God's kingdom on earth. To be more precise: *The purpose of the church is to be God's missionary people in the world.* Missions is not an afterthought in the mind of God. There is no partnership in Christ without partnership in missions.

But is this really our top priority? In his book *The Household of God*, Leslie Newbigin rightly criticizes the thinking in many of our churches (p. 165):

> It is taken for granted that the missionary obligation is one that has to be met AFTER the needs of the home have been fully met; that existing gains have to be thoroughly consolidated before we go further afield; that the world-wide church has to be built up with the same sort of prudent enterprise.

Such thinking is a sin against the truth. The church is to be missionary because that is its divine design. Thus it is vital that the church be other-worldly and this-worldly *at the very same time.* Only as our congregations intentionally live out their nature as God's missionary people will the church begin to emerge to become what Christ is creating it to be. This missionary focus of the church as a *sent* group of people is stressed in Johannes Blauw's classic work *The Missionary Nature of the Church* (pp. 121-22):

> If one wants to maintain a specific theological meaning of the term mission as "foreign mission," its significance is, in my opinion, that it keeps calling the Church to think over its essential nature as a community *sent* forth into the world. Seen in that light missionary work is not just one of its activities, but *the criterion for all its activities....* It is exactly by going outside itself that the Church *is* itself and comes to itself.

I agree wholeheartedly with this statement. Missions is the inevitable and indispensable expression of the church's essential nature as a fellowship of Christ's disciples. The church is not a hierarchy or an institution but a people in community whose mission is to spread the rule of Christ. The purpose of the Body of Christ is to make Jesus visible in the world. In fact, in the present age the church is uniquely the instrument of the kingdom of God in the world. Thus service to the kingdom means service to the world through missional activity.

Church and Kingdom

There is great practical significance to this truth. It means that local congregations must live out their spiritual life not only as church but also as God's people in the world. Our calling and assignment is to preach the Gospel of the kingdom to the whole world (Mark 16:15). Once again, missiologist Leslie Newbigin captures the essence of what I am trying to say (*The Gospel in a Pluralistic Society*, pp. 232-33):

> [I]t has to be said that there can be no going back to the "Constantinian" era. It will only be by movements that begin with the local congregation in which the reality of the new creation is present, known, and experienced, and from which men and women will go into every sector of public life to claim it for Christ, to unmask the illusions which have remained hidden and to expose all areas of public life to the illumination of the gospel. But this will happen as and when local congregations renounce an introverted concern for their own life, and recognize that they exist for the sake of those who are not members, as sign, instrument, and foretaste of God's redeeming grace for the whole life of society.

Christian Archy

What Newbigin is saying is vitally important. Congregations must no longer follow an introverted, self-serving agenda. Our priority must be to become the King's servants in the world. Local congregations must begin to see themselves as satellite offices of the kingdom of God. Each member must consider him- or herself a strategic player in missionary work as both salt and light. Jesus spoke only of the salt *of the earth* and the light *of the world.* Both elements must be dispersed if they are to be effective. Churches must get out of the saltshaker – out of their self-centered fellowships that negate their very reason for existence. Even Christian marriage has a higher purpose than marital happiness and compatibility. Believing husbands and wives must be partners in the Gospel (Phil. 1:5), intentionally creating perspectives, attitudes, priorities, and goals that are in keeping with the Great Commission of Jesus. The same truth can be extended to our families, churches, and seminaries. As members of Christ's missionary Body, our purpose is to build up the community of the saints in mission to the world.

This missionary perspective will color, direct, and motivate everything the church does. I am reminded of what a friend once told me: "My church spends 35,000 dollars annually on Sunday School quarterlies, money that in my opinion could be much better spent on global missions. Yet few in our church have had the courage to suggest that our investment is a misuse of the Lord's resources." Evangelist Tom Skinner once said, "Let's be honest. We tithe to ourselves." What he meant is that most of the money we contribute to the offering plate is used for facilities and programs designed for ourselves and our families. Very little is dedicated to evangelism or social action, whether in our communities or in the rest of the world.

It all boils down to priorities. And there is absolutely no reason why our priorities should not change. We must ask ourselves, "How would God have us use the resources he has given us to have the greatest possible impact on the kingdom?" In practical terms, this might mean using the Bible instead of quarterlies in our Sunday School classes. It could mean renting a facility to meet in rather than building an expensive sanctuary. It will certainly mean using all of our resources with a sense of global responsibility. As Paul said, stewardship requires us to ask how we can use the resources God has entrusted to us more equitably (see 2 Cor. 8:13-15). Each of us must examine our lifestyles for wasted resources that could be invested in the kingdom. We must become better stewards of our time, budgets, homes, and physical resources. Some time ago a woman contacted Becky and me about sending us gifts for Ethiopia instead of giving Christmas presents to her grandchildren. The gifts were made out in their names! What would happen if 60 million American evangelicals did the same thing and gave presents to Jesus every Christmas? This is the kind of creative planning that is required if we are to respond to the challenges of global missions.

This readjustment process does not mean falling into the trap of legalism. It does not mean establishing additional "programs." It is the Holy Spirit, through the Word of God, who must be at work so that we may see what the church must become as it emerges from its cocoon and into ministry in the world. Unfortunately, trained seminarians are not always eager to assist their congregations to think about their missionary commitments. It is far easier to maintain the status quo than to involve all members of the church in the work of a missionary community. But ministry is the work of the church among *its entire membership* and never the exclusive responsibility of ordained ministers. I strongly suspect that only a grassroots movement in many of our congregations will be able to successfully conquer the forces of inertia. But if we take seriously the idea that every member is a minister and that the clergy-laity distinction is unscriptural, then it follows that we cannot limit theological education to a select few. Ministerial training belongs to and must actively involve the whole people of God.

And what should be the goal of our training? *The people must be trained in serving rather being served.* This means that theological education must be "inside-out." Its purpose is to equip God's people for works of service to the world. The goal is to teach, train, encourage, apprentice, and mobilize the people of God for the work of the ministry. Church leaders, whether seminary trained or not, will be deemed "successful" to the degree that the church becomes the missionary people of God. Leaders will be judged, not by their rhetorical prowess, but to the degree to which the people's spiritual gifts are expressed in ministry. Pastors are not called into ministry any more than any other church member. But they *are* charged with the solemn obligation of preparing God's people for works of service (Eph. 4:11-12).

Notice that I have said nothing about leadership as administration or management. Lawrence O. Richards and Clyde Hoeldtke correctly point out in their book *A Theology of Church Leadership* (p. 6) that the church "is a living body of the living Jesus. Since we are part of a body, not an institution, the task of body leaders must be distinctively different from the management task of institutional leaders." Leadership, thus defined, calls for people who will be catalysts to mobilize the people of God for mission in the world. These people lead best when they themselves model, illustrate, and perform service to the world. On the other hand, leaders must be wary of assuming a "clergy" role in ministry. One reason the so-called laity are so passive is because leaders have made "ministry" and "missions" the professional roles of a few ordained people. Leaders lead best when they do the tasks *and* teach others to do them. Effective ministry calls for participation by *all*.

The fields are white unto harvest. So said Jesus. Let us, then, ask the Lord of the harvest to grant us laborers. Jesus did not come to condemn the world but to save it (John 3:17). He forces us to reexamine our priorities as the people of God. Are leaders directing the laborers in an efficient and fruitful way? Are they themselves going out into the fields? Is the Gospel the criterion for all of our activities? Are we willing to lay down our lives for the world? Have we forgotten the purpose for which the treasure of the Gospel was entrusted to us? Have we kept it wrapped up and buried in the ground? To such unprofitable servants Jesus said, "You wicked and lazy servant! You ought to have invested my money with the bankers, and at my coming I should have received what was my own with interest." The Gospel has not been entrusted to us to be buried in the ground.

Jesus' Great Commission is the church's marching orders. By this I do not mean to imply that missionary activity is something onerous. To be sure, it takes up a great deal of one's time, energy, and (if one is self-supporting) financial resources. But by no means is it an occasion for self-pity! Again, no one has put this better than missiologist Leslie Newbigin, to whom I must give the final word in this chapter (*The Gospel in a Pluralist Society*, p. 116):

There has been a long tradition which sees the mission of the Church primarily as obedience to a command. It has been customary to speak of "the missionary mandate." This way of putting the matter is certainly not without justification, and yet it seems to me that it misses the point. It tends to make mission a burden rather than a joy, to make it part of the law rather than part of the gospel. If one looks at the New Testament evidence one gets another impression. Missions begins with a kind of explosive joy. The news that the rejected and crucified Jesus is alive is something that cannot possibly be suppressed. It must be told.

Chapter 5:

The Power of the Powerless

One of the most effective aspects of teaching is the exemplary story. Some people are to be admired and imitated, while others are to studied, not for their imitation, but for their value as negative examples. This is how our character is largely formed. "Example is better than precept," we say. Thus, "Who is my neighbor?" is a question that is best answered by an exemplary tale. The story of the Good Samaritan is famous because of that fact. Its meaning is explicit and clear. And no one doubts that Jesus himself is the protagonist of the story and the model of unconditional love. It is he "who loved me and gave himself for me" (Gal. 2:20).

That is also the meaning behind the magnificent Christ hymn of Philippians 2:5-11. Here we find inspiration for that form of *agape* love that is so characteristically exercised within the church as well as toward those on the outside. It springs from the ethics of Jesus himself, an ethic that is both commanded (John 13:34) and enabled (John 15:12). This radically selfless character of divine *agape* is seen most clearly in its concern for the good of others. Jesus is the object of the Father's love, and he in turn loved his own disciples both collectively and individually (Mary, Martha, Lazarus, etc.). The story of Jesus – his incarnation, his selfless life, his example of consistently loving behavior, his death and resurrection "for us" – was the definitive expression of God's love for his creation. Paul describes this as the love of God himself in his concern for humans (Rom. 5:8). The essence of the kingdom of God is a response to and imitation of this love as manifested through Jesus Christ. His followers share both the bearing and the destiny of the Suffering Servant. That is to say, the humility of Jesus is to be the normal disposition of the Christian. This thought is not limited, of course, to the Christ hymn of Philippians 2 but lies behind Paul's words in 2 Corinthians 8:9 that Christ, "although he was rich, became poor for your sakes, so that you by his poverty might become rich."

But this raises a question: If a model is needed, why not limit ourselves to Jesus? Why should the New Testament constantly appeal to the example of his followers, whether Timothy (Phil. 2:19-24), Epaphroditus (Phil. 2:25-30), Paul (Phil. 2:17-18), or any number of other paradigmatic figures? The answer appears to be that, so far as the imitation of Christ is concerned, we humans are deeply affected by the lives of men and women whose generous and charitable character alert us to the real meaning of love. There are numerous passages in the New Testament in which believers are exalted for their Christ-like behavior and whose lives presuppose Jesus' teaching about his upside-down kingdom. The vision of this future-yet-already-here kingdom is a powerful motive for acting in ways that will direct outsiders to the signs of its dawning.

Paul could properly describe this motive as the "mind of Christ" (Phil. 2:5) in his famous Christological hymn. Heavy weather has been made of this passage by modern critics, who have assumed that it derives from a pre- or non-Pauline source. But in fact the passage need be no more than a concise formulation of what the apostle has spelled out in greater detail in other places. Paul is not saying anything new when he characterizes Jesus as the perfect man who achieves for humanity through his suffering and death what was lost through Adam's sin and pride (see Rom. 5:12-21; 1 Cor. 15:21-22). What *is* new here is how the apostle uses the example of Jesus as an illustration of the unity and humility that characterize true Christian discipleship. A study of the structure of Philippians reveals that 2:5-11 is nothing but the illustration and application of 2:1-4, a central passage that shows how necessary humility is to Christian unity (see my essays, "Paul and Christian Unity," "On the Authorship of Philippians 2:5-11," and "The Discourse Structure of Philippians"). But there is more. For in subsequent paragraphs of the letter (2:17-18, 2:19-24, and 2:25-30) the "humility" of Christ is exemplified in three flesh-and-blood persons, all of whom were known to the Philippians. Clearly Paul recognizes in himself, Timothy, and Epaphroditus the same "mind" that characterized the Savior. The effect is to indicate that sacrificial service for others in the cause of the Gospel is the normative strategy for all Christians who inhabit the kingdom.

It is in this perspective that we can best approach Paul's stirring affirmation that God desires us to love our fellow human beings, regardless of the consequences (Rom. 12:9-21). As I argued earlier, neither Paul nor Jesus propounded a new social movement that would use government coercion to attain its goals. The essence of New Testament teaching regarding the kingdom of God is not to command obedience to moral rules but to incline us towards behavior motivated and prompted by Jesus' scandalous death. However much else is uncertain about Jesus of Nazareth, this surely is known: he placed more emphasis upon social *outlook* than upon social *legislation*. The ideals he espoused are attitudes rather than programs or policies. Just how they are to be expressed *politically* will be a matter of opinion. But no one can claim that Jesus was a political teacher or that he would have supported Christianized politics. Hence pacifist politicians can hardly claim the support of Jesus for their views, for even if we grant that war as an institution is opposed to the spirit of Jesus, this pacifistic attitude does not determine the technique by which love of enemy should be expressed. The same Jesus who said "Do not resist evil" also thought of himself as binding the strong man and advised his disciples to buy swords (Luke 22:35-38). In no case should we subordinate the principle of love to a casuistic legalism justified by appeals to sayings of Jesus that were never intended to be political. He himself preferred death to political agitation. His kingdom was not of this world. If we desire the sanction of Jesus for any form of political involvement we must appeal not to any of his specific sayings but to the spirit of his teachings. It is possible to show that many of Paul's teachings carry with them a similar implication. His is a vision of a kind of society in which love and non-retaliation would be the norm. But there is very little here about what form of social legislation might be necessary to ensure moral behavior of this kind (see my essay, "The Pauline Love Command: Structure, Style, and Ethics in Romans 12:9-21").

We must have the courage to say flatly that human archys are nothing less than the contemporary resurrection of the pharisaic ethic. It is the way of the cross (*via crucis*) that the disciple must follow with no other motive than that the Master bids it. It was he who refused to conquer the kingdoms of this world by the means proposed by the Tempter. To limit Christianity to social activism would betray Jesus because he never placed his spirituality in the service of an immediate political end.

This may be the nub of the matter for many of us: our traditional patterns of religious and political scalp-hunting are the very things that prevent the Holy Spirit from penetrating the stubborn patterns of our lives. And the more sincere and humble the activist is, the firmer is his or her hold on other people – and therefore the more dangerous. We are so accustomed to the church having its ethics commissions and public policy boards that we find it practically impossible to imagine the church without them. It is well to remember that neither Paul nor any of the other apostles ever challenged the political status quo. They never saw and never imagined a church with people rushing on their feet to keep the political machinery going. The church can overcome this false allegiance only by returning to the basic doctrine of Christ's incarnation and his utter devotion to the kingdom of God.

Once again, we can put the point in terms of Christian Archy. The kingdom of God belongs not to the powerful and religious, but to the poor and childlike humble. The test is simple: How much do you really serve the world without religious and political machinations? It is only when we become active in obedience to the Suffering Servant that the ministry of reconciliation (1 Cor. 5:17) is seen in its true meaning and has its full freedom of operation.

Chapter 6:

Conclusion

In this book I have argued that there will be no adequate progress made in the church until it begins to take seriously the doctrine of the kingdom of God. It is fundamental to the New Testament that God does not need the wisdom and power of our earthly archys to accomplish his purposes. We must, therefore, examine ourselves and ruthlessly ask if we are willing to pay the price for such a revolution in our philosophy. The church in its most serious thinking must come to grips with its false utopias and its failure to extend the Creator-King's rule into every aspect of daily life.

This will demand a serious reorientation of our thinking at every level. It may be that much of the trouble will be found in the inadequacy of our denominational structures and goals. We may need to rethink whether we are truly kingdom-focused or merely program-driven. To put things bluntly, a good many of our young pastors have reached a tipping point when it comes to redundant and ineffective ecclesiastical structures. And, let it be said, there are church leaders and denominational bureaucrats who sometimes forget that the expansion of the kingdom into the whole of creation is the first concern of the church. It is not clear whether the younger generation of pastors will forsake denominational affiliations *en masse*. But it does seem certain that a good many of them will continue to question the misplaced priorities of their predecessors. They have had quite enough of resolutions that seem to take place with tiresome regularity at annual religious conventions. The passing of resolutions merely deceives people into thinking that they have achieved something, whereas not the slightest difference is made. The congregations themselves are left largely untouched and uninfluenced by such resolutions.

Whether we accept it or not, whether the church makes it central or not, whether it seems true or not, Jesus taught that powerless love is the only basis upon which to build the kingdom. Followers of Jesus who claim this perspective as their own may differ as to methods, but they will always "seek first the kingdom of God" and forsake all forms of demagoguery and manipulation. The biblical Christ knew unparalleled social compassion. His was a theology of hope. Within the movement he began there may be different theologies and practices, but these all will be controlled and guided by that central attitude which Jesus described and uncompromisingly embodied: Love of God, and love of neighbor. There is, in fact, no other way to live if we are to see God (Matt. 5:8), enjoy the treasures that are insusceptible to rust and moths (Matt.

Conclusion

6:19-20), and sit at the heavenly banquet with Jesus (Rev. 15:5-10).

It is imperative that we no longer use intellectual excuses in order to evade our responsibilities as disciples of Jesus. In him we find a true Revolutionary who is capable of saving the world without using coercion or violence of any kind. Let us, then, make it our aim in life to exhibit Christ's cross-love in anticipation of that day when the Husband will come for his Bride, and together they will rule over their vast kingdom (Rev. 22:5).

For Further Reading

Augsburger, David. *Dissident Discipleship*. Grand Rapids: Brazos, 2006.

Balmer, Randall. *Thy Kingdom Come*. New York: Basic Books, 2006.

Bonhoeffer, Dietrich. *The Cost of Discipleship*. New York: Simon & Shuster, 1995.

Black, David Alan. "Paul and Christian Unity: A Formal Analysis of Philippians 2:1-4." *Journal of the Evangelical Theological Society* 28 (1985) 299-308.

Black, David Alan. *Paul, Apostle of Weakness*. New York: Lang, 1984.

Black, David Alan. "The Authorship of Philippians 2:6-11: Some Literary-Critical Observations." *Criswell Theological Review* 2 (1988) 269-89.

Black, David Alan. "The Discourse Structure of Philippians: A Study in Textlinguistics." *Novum Testamentum* 37 (1995) 16-49.

Black, David Alan. *The Jesus Paradigm*. Pensacola, FL: Energion, 2009.

Black, David Alan. "The Pauline Love Command: Structure, Style, and Ethics in Romans 12:9-21." *Filologia Neotestamentaria* 2 (1989) 3-22.

Blauw, Johannes. *The Missionary Nature of the Church.* New York: McGraw-Hill, 1962.

Boyd, Gregory. *The Myth of a Christian Nation.* Grand Rapids: Zondervan, 2005.

Claiborne, Shane. *The Irresistible Revolution.* Grand Rapids: Zondervan, 2006.

Durnbaugh, Donald F. *The Believers' Church.* New York: Macmillan, 1968.

Eller, Vernard. *Christian Anarchy.* Eugene, OR: Wipf and Stock, 1999.

Ellul, Jacques. *Anarchy and Christianity.* Grand Rapids: Eerdmans, 1991.

Ellul, Jacques. *Living Faith.* San Francisco: Harper & Row, 1983.

Ellul, Jacques. *The Politics of God and the Politics of Man.* Grand Rapids: Eerdmans, 1972.

For Further Reading

Ellul, Jacques. *The Presence of the Kingdom*. Colorado Springs, CO: Helmers & Howard, 1989.

Ellul, Jacques. *The Subversion of Christianity*. Grand Rapids: Eerdmans, 1986.

Ellul, Jacques. *Violence*. New York: Seabury, 1969.

Hauerwas, Stanley. *The Peaceable Kingdom*. Notre Dame: University of Notre Dame, 1983.

Kierkegaard, Søren. *Provocations*. New York: Orbis, 2002.

Kraybill, Donald B. *The Upside-Down Kingdom*. Scottdale, PA: Herald Press, 2003.

McKnight, Scot. *The Jesus Creed*. Grand Rapids: Brewster, MA: Paraclete, 2004.

Newbigin, Leslie. *The Gospel in a Pluralistic Society*. London: SPCK, 1989.

Newbigin, Leslie. *The Household of God*. New York: Friendship, 1954.

Phillips, Kevin. *American Theocracy*. New York: Penguin, 2006.

Christian Archy

Richards, Lawrence O. and Clyde Hoeldtke. *A Theology of Church Leadership*. Grand Rapids: Zondervan, 1980.

Snyder, Howard A. *The Community of the King*. Downers Grove: InterVarsity. 2004.

Yoder, John Howard. *The Politics of Jesus*. Grand Rapids: Eerdmans, 1994.

Yoder, John Howard. *The Priestly Kingdom*. Notre Dame: University of Notre Dame, 2001.

Yohannan, K. P. *The Road to Reality*. Carrolton, TX: GFA Books, 2004.

Topics and Persons Index

American flag...3
Anabaptists...11
Archy...1, 4ff., 9, 11ff., 32
Blauw, Johannes..18
Body of Christ...2, 18
Christian Anarchy...1, 3, 5ff., 11f., 14
Christian Left...6
Christian Right..6
Christus Victor...2
Church...................................1ff., viff., 11f., 14f., 17ff., 22ff., 27, 32ff.
Churchly archys...8, 12
Clergy..22f.
Colonization..15
Communism...15
Complementarianism...15
Conservative..5
Cross...3, 5f., 15, 31, 35
Desacralization...8, 11
Discipleship...29
Earthly archys...7, 15, 33
Egalitarianism...15
Eller, Vernard..1ff., 5ff., 11, 13f.
Ellul, Jacques...1ff., 8, x, 14f.
Epaphroditus..28, 30
Establishment archys..11
Ethics...27, 31f.
Free Church...11
Glory...viii
Great Commission...vii, 20, 24
Hoeldtke, Clyde...23
Holy Spirit...2, 8, 22, 32
Homeschool...12ff.
Human archys...6f., 11, 31
Ideology...6
Kierkegaard, Søren..1ff.
Kingdom..1f., ivff., 8ff., 15, 17ff., 28ff.
Kingdom of God................................5f., viiif., 15, 18, 20, 28, 30, 32ff.

41

Legalism..22, 31
Liberal...5, 7, 15
Magisterial Reformers..11
Marriage...20
Missional activity...18
Missionary..17f., 20, 22ff.
Missions...17f., 20, 22f., 25
Nationalism...1
New Testament..2f., viii, x, 12, 25, 28ff., 33
Newbigin, Leslie..17, 19f., 24
Paul...28ff.
Politics..1, 6f., 14, 30
Richards, Lawrence O...23
Skinner, Tom..20
Suffering..viii, 29
Suffering Servant...28, 32
Theological education..22
Timothy...28, 30
Tithe...21
Via crucis..31

Scripture Index

Matthew 5:8..34
Matthew 6:19-20...34
Luke 22:35-38...31
John 3:17..24
John 13:34..27
John 15:12..27
Romans 5:8..28
Romans 12:9-21..30, 31
Romans 5:12-21...29
1 Corinthians 2:2..vii
1 Corinthians 5:17..32
1 Corinthians 15:21-22...29
2 Corinthians 8:9..28
2 Corinthians 8:13-15...21
Ephesians 6:1-4..13
Ephesians 4:11-12..23
Philippians 1:5..20
Philippians 2..27, 28
Philippians 2:1-4...29
Philippians 2:5..29
Philippians 2:5-11...27, 29
Philippians 2:17-18...28, 29
Philippians 2:19-24...28, 30
Philippians 2:25-30...28, 30
Revelation 14:4-5..viii
Revelation 15:5-10..35
Revelation 22:5...35